# Reform Medicaid First

# Reform Medicaid First
## Laying the Foundation for
## National Health Care Reform

Thomas W. Grannemann
and Mark V. Pauly

The AEI Press

*Publisher for the American Enterprise Institute*
WASHINGTON, D.C.

To order call toll free 1-800-462-6420 or
1-717-794-3800. For all other inquiries please contact the AEI Press, 1150
Seventeenth Street, N.W., Washington, D.C. 20036 or call 1-800-862-5801.

Library of Congress Cataloging-in-Publication Data

Grannemann, Thomas W.
    Reform Medicaid first: laying the foundation for national health care
    reform / Thomas W. Grannemann and Mark V. Pauly.
    p.; cm.

Includes bibliographical references.
    ISBN-13: 978-0-8447-4316-5
    ISBN-10: 0-8447-4316-X

    1. Medicaid. 2. Health care reform—United States. 3. Medical policy—
United States. I. Pauly, Mark V., 1941- II. Title. [DNLM: 1. Medicaid. 2.
Health Care Reform—United States. 3. National Health Programs—United
States. W 250 AA1 G759r 2009]

    RA412.4.G73 2009
    368.4'200973—dc22

                                                        2009022003
13 12  11  10  09          1  2  3  4  5

# Contents

# List of Illustrations

# Introduction:
# Why Medicaid First?

Beneath the swirling surface of the current debate over national health-care reform lie some fundamental problems with the existing system—problems that must be recognized and addressed as part of any credible reform effort. Some of the more troublesome of these are legacies of the current Medicaid program and its distinct manifestations in the fifty states and other jurisdictions. While some aspects of Medicaid present barriers to implementing a new health insurance program, the Medicaid program also presents opportunities to make fundamental changes necessary to any genuine reform of our health-care system. Policymakers should incorporate Medicaid reform into the first stage of any national health-care reform effort. Here's why.

First, *Medicaid reform is a politically feasible first step* that could appeal to voter-taxpayers by providing high-value services to those who need them most. Public support is critical to any expansion of publicly funded or subsidized medical care. Reflecting on the history and politics of Medicaid, we see clear evidence of an altruistic component in voter support for the program—a willingness to pay for services to others in greater need than oneself. This willingness, however, has definite limits. Survey results and evidence from the Medicaid program choices of fifty states suggest that reforms involving significant new spending may not be popular with the public. At the same time, Medicaid builds on natural inclinations to feel more altruistic toward people who are closer at hand by providing federal assistance that encourages taxpayers to support Medicaid benefits for people in their own states, which may be

1

more satisfying than endorsing additional spending on broad-based national subsidies. If the first steps in reform focus on the types of expansions for the poor and near-poor that have the greatest support from voter-taxpayers, we may over time see greater voter willingness to support measures reaching the larger numbers of uninsured people who do not have low incomes and are not at high risk.

Second, interstate *disparities in Medicaid eligibility and benefits* within the Medicaid program itself are perhaps among the most troubling characteristics of our current health-care system. While some degree of interstate variation is reasonable, Medicaid currently provides a quite uneven foundation upon which to build any national plan that would address the problem of the uninsured. These disparities are substantial when measured by Medicaid payments per poor person (see figure I-1) and somewhat less but still substantial if adjusted for interstate differences in cost of living and geographic differences in medical costs (see figure I-2).[1] Any new national program aimed toward ensuring uniform access to care by complementing Medicaid would have to cover very large numbers of uninsured in some states and fill comparatively small gaps in others. The alternatives are to make Medicaid itself more equitable or to replace it with a more equitable national program, either of which would directly involve major changes in Medicaid and other programs for the populations it serves. In this regard, Medicaid's unequal benefits present a barrier that must be addressed prior to, or as part of, any broader reform effort.

Third, interstate *inequities in the distribution of federal health-care dollars* present a kind of political barrier to reaching consensus on broader national reform. These inequities are not well recognized or broadly understood by policymakers or the public. The current Medicaid program directs a disproportionate share of federal dollars to a small number of high-benefit states, many of which are (in an apparent inconsistency with program goals) higher-income states. The natural self-interest of these states in protecting their relatively high federal funding levels can make it difficult for legislators to reach a consensus on any reform that would redirect resources

FIGURE I-1

MEDICAID PAYMENTS PER PERSON BELOW FEDERAL
POVERTY LEVEL, FEDERAL FISCAL YEAR 2007

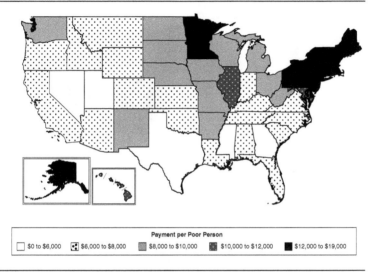

**Payment per Poor Person**

☐ $0 to $6,000　▦ $6,000 to $8,000　▦ $8,000 to $10,000　▦ $10,000 to $12,000　■ $12,000 to $19,000

SOURCES: Computed using data from U.S. Census Bureau, *Current Population Survey*, 2008 Annual Social and Economic Supplement, table POV 46, Poverty Status by State, http:// pubdb3.census.gov/macro/032008/pov/new46_100125_01.htm; and Urban Institute and Kaiser Commission on Medicaid and the Uninsured estimates, based on data from Centers for Medicare and Medicaid Services-64 reports, March 2009, reported on www.statehealthfacts.org figures for "Total Medicaid Spending" (http://www.statehealthfacts.org/comparemaptable.jsp? ind=177&cat=4).

NOTE: Total federal and state medical payments for FY 2007 include disproportionate share hospital (DSH) payments and exclude administrative costs.

toward the current low-benefit states, as any plan with more-uniform eligibility and benefits nationally would need to do. Any national reform directed at reducing the numbers of uninsured will need to correct this imbalance in federal funding, or it risks reinforcing the economic and political forces that sustain the current pattern of the uninsured across states. In this context, Medicaid's uneven federal funding should be recognized and addressed up front as part of any reform package—and an unwillingness to do so represents a real barrier to meaningful reform.

FIGURE I-2

REAL MEDICAID PAYMENTS PER PERSON BELOW
125 PERCENT OF COST OF LIVING–ADJUSTED FEDERAL
POVERTY LEVEL, FEDERAL FISCAL YEAR 2007

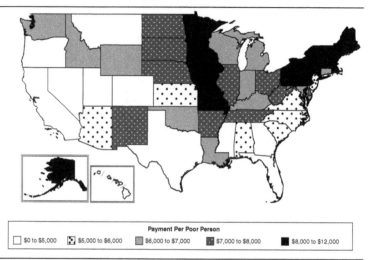

| | | Payment Per Poor Person | | |
|---|---|---|---|---|
| ☐ $0 to $5,000 | ▓ $5,000 to $6,000 | ▓ $6,000 to $7,000 | ▓ $7,000 to $8,000 | ■ $8,000 to $12,000 |

SOURCES: Computed using data from U.S. Census Bureau, *Current Population Survey*, 2008 Annual Social and Economic Supplement, table POV 46 (data interpolated from http://pubdb3 .census.gov/macro/032008/pov/new46_100125_01.htm and http://pubdb3.census.gov/macro/ 032008/pov/new46_135150_01.htm); Urban Institute and Kaiser Commission on Medicaid and the Uninsured estimates, based on data from Centers for Medicare and Medicaid Services-64 reports, March 2009, reported on www.statehealthfacts.org, figures for "Total Medicaid Spending" (http://www.statehealthfacts.org/comparemaptable.jsp?ind= 177&cat=4); and MERIC state cost of living index at www.missourieconomy.org (http://www.missourieconomy.org/ indicators/cost_of_living/index.stm).

NOTES: Total federal and state medical payments for FY 2007 include disproportionate share hospital (DSH) payments and exclude administrative costs; payments are deflated by average of physician practice cost index; number of poor is estimated by adjusting 125 percent of the federal poverty level (FPL) by the Missouri Economic Research Information Center (MERIC) state cost of living index.

Fourth, *any new plan must mesh with Medicaid.* A new plan to expand insurance coverage to lower-income workers should be integrated or coordinated as well as possible with coverage of the poor (and those with fluctuating low incomes who cycle in and out of Medicaid eligibility) by Medicaid and the State Children's Health Insurance Program (SCHIP or, more recently, CHIP) to ensure continuity in the level of public subsidy and, thus, equity up and down the beneficiary income distribution. This objective of "vertical equity" requires filling the gaps and reducing the unevenness in Medicaid benefits for the poor across states ahead of any national program to extend coverage up the income distribution to low-income workers and other uninsured. Attention should be paid with any new program to make it mesh with Medicaid in its different forms across states

Fifth, Medicaid reform may presently be the *best use of limited funds*. President Barack Obama's budget calls for a down payment on health reform. This down payment could well be used to fix Medicaid by bringing basic eligibility and benefits per person in the low-income, low-benefit states (which is where most of the uninsured are, anyway) up closer to the national average. Doing so even within the existing Medicaid framework would be a more equitable use of limited funds than broader, partial solutions directed at subsidizing persons further up the income distribution or extending coverage in selected higher-income states, which have been the targets of many recent reform proposals.

Sixth, comprehensive *near-universal coverage* will only be affordable with a more cost-effective health-care system, which *may be years away*. Quality-enhancing innovations such as electronic medical records, e-prescribing, preventive care, pay for performance, and evidence-based guidelines have not yet been shown to save much money and, from what we have seen, Americans will need to make sacrifices to get costs under control before they are comfortable with supporting near-universal coverage. Substantial reductions in the uninsured may, in fact, be undertaken at current levels of cost and cost growth, but full and stable near-universal coverage will require a rate of spending growth tolerable to the general population. So long as medical costs are growing more rapidly than Americans' incomes, it will be hard to get voters to willingly mandate or subsidize coverage for all. Consequently, Medicaid reform, in concert with Medicare reform and cost containment efforts in the private sector, is needed to rationalize the flow of resources into the health-care sector.

In short, there are some fundamental systemic problems with current Medicaid, CHIP, and government health-care safety-net programs. We have neither the resources nor the public support to provide universal national health care without effective cost containment, which realistically is years away, and uncertain at that. Proceeding toward national reform without dealing with the shortcomings of existing programs will perpetuate the unequal distribution of federal health-care resources and further entrench economic and political interests in the imbalance. In contrast, reforming Medicaid first (or as an early component of a broader reform plan) could address the most pressing problems of the current system, help establish principles of equity that should form the basis of any national health-care reform plans, and, in conjunction with Medicare and other payers, help bring about reform of the health-care delivery system. This is the only way we will be able to make universal coverage affordable, politically supportable, and financially sustainable in the long run.

Medicaid should, by rights, be squarely on the national agenda, and an integral part of any reasonable national health-care reform plan. Changes in Medicaid will be needed first. To try to wrap health reform around the current Medicaid system without changes in Medicaid itself would very likely present serious implementation difficulties or result in a reformed system that at least maintains, and may well aggravate, present inequities in the distribution of benefits and federal financing. If resources are not immediately available to go all the way to universal coverage, then fixing the problems with Medicaid is a logical place to start getting the best value for the health reform dollars that are available in the near term. Even if resources are adequate to go further, it still makes sense to make Medicaid the first step in reform.

# 1

# Medicaid Reflects Public Choices

Medicaid spending reflects public choices, through the democratic process, about what voters are willing to pay to provide medical-care services to the poor. The local preferences apparent in voter-taxpayers' concern for their states' own residents are at the heart of the rationale for Medicaid as a federal–state program. Medicaid's state-level implementation and administration take into account people's greater willingness to support public funding of medical care for the nearby poor. Through Medicaid programs in fifty states, the District of Columbia, and U.S. territories, voters can demonstrate their differing levels of generosity and, accordingly, do more or less in their own communities without having to get the agreement of all others in the country. Real-world politics is, of course, more complex, with interest groups and elites having more influence than voter-taxpayers. When votes are traded, some elected representatives may accept less favorable federal Medicaid funding in return for other subsidies or benefits for interests within their states. Still, consideration of local altruism will be important in any effort to reshape the Medicaid program or create any new public program, as politicians in a democracy cannot neglect the underlying interests of voters and the interest they express in providing adequate medical coverage for the poor and others.

This local concern is paradoxically, in some cases, at odds with broader voter concern for the well-being of the poor nationally, as is apparent in the unease of many observers with the inequality in Medicaid benefits for the poor across states. Some proposals for a unified national health program for the poor would involve the creation of a single standard for eligibility and benefits at the national level. Depending on the level of public subsidies, a uniform national approach to reform could help equalize benefits across states, but it might also result (in many states) in lower benefits than are provided in the current federal–state Medicaid system. In a model of public choices about Medicaid spending, which we discuss elsewhere, we suggest that such an equal-standards approach would not take account of voters' greater willingness to provide benefits to those in their own communities.[2] As a result, a uniform national plan could, in the long run, have the unintended effect of lowering overall average levels of benefits and reducing the economic efficiency of the program in providing the right level of public goods. Although voters could step up and support a benefit level higher than the current average, the public choice model suggests that, without the ability to direct their taxes to support their local communities, they may perceive less value in the tax dollars spent and tend toward a new equilibrium national level of benefits that is below the current average Medicaid level.

Health-care reform planners should keep in mind the distinct role of Medicaid and medical safety-net programs in the United States. The motivation for these programs has been altruistic interest in providing assistance to those truly in need, which distinguishes Medicaid both from Medicare (from which most taxpayers expect to benefit themselves someday) and from employer-based insurance, which is viewed as part of the reward for work. It also distinguishes Medicaid from the health-care programs of many European countries, which claim to base their programs on "solidarity" and design them to benefit all within their national borders. In the Medicaid experience, altruistic motivations of voter-taxpayers to support public financing of care for the poor appear to fall off as the program increasingly benefits higher-income groups that are more able to bear the cost of their own medical care. Voter valuations of program expenditures are subject to the law of diminishing returns as recipient income rises. Evidence from Medicaid and SCHIP/CHIP suggests that motivation to fund care from state taxes drops rather quickly as one goes up the recipient income scale (hence the need for enhanced federal matching to encourage CHIP expansions to nonpoor children). Therefore, unless we were to see a transforming shift in voter preferences, we would not expect voters, even in a reformed system, to willingly pay much more than they currently do to support people with incomes above the Medicaid and CHIP eligibility levels. Most additional funding to expand coverage to the working uninsured would need to come from the workers themselves, their employers, or federal sources.

To reflect the nature of American altruism, then, program designs to cover the uninsured should distinguish the truly poor, who simply cannot afford to pay much for their own care, from those workers who can contribute significantly to the cost of their coverage but find it challenging to do so. Part of the design problem is that there is no bright line between these groups, even though they might best be served by distinct types of public programs. Because others' altruistic motives (especially with respect to local altruism) are high and beneficiary ability to pay low for the lowest income groups, there are clear advantages, from a public choice perspective, of serving such people in a federal–state program such as Medicaid or CHIP. However, this view of the nature of local altruism suggests the objective of serving households that are somewhat better off might best be met through a separate program without state funding, using instead a mix of employer contributions, when available, and federal subsidies (direct and through tax deductions and credits).

For this reason, it is probably unwise to combine Medicaid with any new program designed for groups with incomes above currently common CHIP eligibility levels (about 200 percent of the federal poverty level). Policymakers should be very conscious of the need, as one goes up the beneficiary income scale, for policy to reflect declining altruism and increased household ability to pay— and especially their implications for adjusting the subsidy shares of payers to beneficiary income, which in turn may require distinct forms of program administration. (This argument for segmentation is strengthened when one notes that the prevalence of private insurance coverage also increases rapidly as one goes up the income scale, increasing, in turn, the possibility that additional public spending will supplant or crowd out private purchase of insurance.) This need to tailor the program structure by beneficiary income segment will be relevant whether policymakers decide to pursue a segmented multiprogram strategy or a single, seamless, uniform national program.

## Public Support for Spending Has Limits

Viewed as resulting from public choices, the Medicaid and CHIP experiences point to six key facts that must be confronted by any major Medicaid reform or broader health-care reform.

- Voters show more support for public spending for coverage of those with the lowest income and/or assets, especially those unable to earn income for themselves (that is, Medicaid's traditional eligibility groups of children, the elderly, and disabled adults).

- U.S. voter-taxpayers appear willing to accept more limits on medical care for others (such as Medicaid recipients and those who use safety-net services) than they do for themselves (as in employer-sponsored plans and Medicare).

- Voters at the state level respond to higher federal matching incentives (with a lower proportion of costs borne by the state) by choosing to broaden eligibility and increase benefits, but those benefits have diminishing marginal value.

- Given the current matching formula, higher-income states are willing to spend more than lower-income states, but they have not generally been willing to sacrifice a larger percentage of taxpayer income to support the state share. (That is, the percentage of taxpayer income paid for the state share of Medicaid has been about the same among high- and low-income states.)

• Among states with high levels of employer coverage, high taxpayer income, and generous federal matching through Medicaid waivers and CHIP, some states (like Massachusetts) are willing to take steps toward near-universal coverage. But other states (like California, Maine, and Illinois) have considered and so far failed to move ahead with such proposals. Time will tell whether stable taxpayer support for near-universal coverage can be attained at the state level, or alternatively, whether some states' unwillingness to support such coverage—even with matching—means that near-universal coverage can only be achieved through a federal program.

• The current level of Medicaid spending (as reflected in federal and state budgets) may be one of our best indicators of voter demand for publicly funded subsidies for the lower-income population. If so, it seems most states, particularly lower-income states, are probably unwilling to spend what would be needed for near-universal-coverage programs, at least at current federal matching rates. While some states might explore such possibilities if Congress and the administration were to offer attractive opportunities, the gap between exploration and enacted legislation is wide. We have always had the opportunity through Medicaid, however, to expand coverage, and to date Congress has taken an incremental approach to expansions—with considerable and often contentious debate at each step. Policymakers contemplating more than an incremental change in the level of public spending in this area should ask themselves what has changed to engender much greater public support, and whether that support will be sustained for years to come at budget time.

Unless something changes to alter these facts, taxpayer support to pay for the implementation of near-universal-coverage programs (even using the Massachusetts model) might be insufficient. In that case, what might raise the level of public willingness to provide the funding needed to achieve closer-to-universal coverage? Here are the factors that might lead voters to support programs with enough public subsidy to do that:

- **Higher incomes brought about by economic growth.** We know that higher income leads to greater spending by taxpayers for those in need. At some point, economic growth and higher incomes may lead taxpayers to support such coverage for all—but, since taxpayers seem willing to spend only a fixed percentage of income on such transfers, this can only occur if economic growth begins to exceed growth in the cost of medical-care services.

- **Lower costs of beneficiary coverage relative to income.** We know that voter-taxpayers respond to the reduction of their costs through federal matching—that is, voters respond to prices. If some other factor could sufficiently reduce the relative costs of coverage (that is, if growth in Medicaid premiums could be pushed well below growth in income), voters might, over time, be willing to expand coverage. Such a change could come from either an unprecedented shift in trend or a reduction in scope of benefits covered (below Medicaid's current comprehensive benefit package). What is really needed here is a lower inflation trend for medical insurance than for taxpayer income. In either case, taxpayers would see a lower cost of providing coverage and higher value in return for their subsidy dollars. Voters might then be predisposed to close the smaller, cheaper-to-fill gap.

- **Increase in taxpayer demand for covering the uninsured.** We know that taxpayer demand for providing coverage through Medicaid varies across states, even across states with the same income levels. If less motivated voters could be persuaded of the value of reducing the number of uninsured—either by stronger appeals to altruism, buttressed by better evidence about the beneficial effects of medical care on the health of the uninsured, or by more evidence that a larger proportion of uninsured worsens the quality of and access to care for those who *are* insured[3]—there might be movement. To accomplish near-universal coverage, voters would need to see greater public value and/or their own self-interest in such a change. While political leadership might change perceptions of the value of medical assistance programs and move people in this direction, underlying voter preferences may be slow to change over time.

None of these shifts seems likely to happen on its own in the near future. Medical spending, for as far back as we have data, has outrun income growth (with only a few, single-year exceptions) in all decades and in all states, and will surely do so in the current economic slowdown. There has as yet been little willingness among politicians (or demand from voters) to have a public conversation about the acceptability of the sacrifices required of the middle class to slow medical spending growth or increase the number of insured households. We are more optimistic for the long run, however, since substantive reform proposals that address both coverage and cost containment are slated for consideration in Congress and may well launch such a conversation about the hard but inevitable choices.

At a macro level, the public choice model suggests that the best route to more universal coverage may be through policies that control medical-care spending while preserving access to the most valuable medical advances. This may entail eliminating care of proven but low value and expensive new technology of positive but unproven expected value. (There are few forms of care that everyone would agree are costly but totally useless, but lots of differences of opinion among doctors and experts on what care is "right," precisely because the evidence is not there.) It may also entail reducing administrative overhead from management and administration in the health-care system. If these things could be done, the increases in persons covered that would move the system toward near-universality might just happen naturally, through more incremental political processes. Completely universal coverage would probably have to include a mandate to bring on board the 5 percent or so of nonpoor persons who will not pay for insurance, but if we could get the uninsured fraction down to that level, then a mandate would be much more feasible to enact and enforce.

At a micro (or incremental) level, any expansion is best directed toward those with incomes just above current Medicaid eligibility levels. Such expansion might be accomplished through subsidies for private voluntary coverage or through expansion of Medicaid-like programs. Among the impediments to taking this step, probably the most important is the so-far unbridged ideological divide between conservatives and liberals. Conservatives may only go as far as accepting subsidies for private insurance that includes considerable beneficiary cost-sharing. Liberals will be seeking broad eligibility with less cost-sharing and more governmental management and control.[4] In a population where many people already have coverage, crowd-out effects may make public expenditures for any program higher than initially expected. Employing some form of cost-sharing, such as co-payments, for the nonpoor (as has been done in Massachusetts) might curb excessive utilization and reduce the total and government share of costs, thereby making the public subsidy of coverage more affordable to voter-taxpayers. If real taxpayer income growth were ever to outstrip the growth in technology-driven medical spending, cost-sharing might then be reduced or eliminated for some lower income levels.

There are those who claim that the gap to be closed is smaller than it looks, and that political support will be forthcoming as the debate progresses. But the gap is substantial in most states, even with presumed offsetting savings.[5] We are skeptical of politicians who claim the taxes needed to close the gap would be small because they have discovered new ways of reducing inefficiency that have thus far eluded the market. Most evidence suggests modest (at best) taxpayer willingness to pay somewhat more to cover others.[6] Moreover, while it would strengthen the case for universal coverage if growth in medical-care spending could be limited, the upper middle class is likely to be unenthusiastic about programs that control *their* spending growth—and effective control programs (based on theory and the experiences of other countries) would almost surely require universal participation in spending limitation.

If our assessment is correct—that American taxpayer-voters (at least those not in high-income states with well-above-average employer-based insurance and a favorable Medicaid waiver) are not yet ready to support voluntarily the public financing needed for close-to-universal uniform coverage—it will be useful to have on hand a proposal for incremental expansion incorporating certain changes in Medicaid. There is not yet, however, a credible map that shows the path to attaining the same goals for the health-care system as a whole. Many people place great hopes on a pathway to reform through care management (such as preventive care, the medical home concept, or new information technology), but none of those methods has been validated as truly cost-saving. We would suggest that more attention be paid to how money shapes delivery of care. This means looking most closely at provider payment issues and incentive-based methods to control the flow of resources into the health-care system and to ensure they go where they will do the most good.[7] We would define that good as directing resources to where they clearly serve to improve the health of beneficiaries, while curbing use of resources in areas where health effects are known to be small. (What to do about the vast gray area in between is more challenging.) This is perhaps the most important principle underlying our suggestions for reforms of the Medicaid program, and for broader reforms as well.

## High-Value Care as a Key to Reform

The kinds of reforms that are most needed are those that will apply strong tools to produce valued outcomes. Such reforms may be best accomplished through Medicaid program financing adjustments. Provider payment and federal financing are the financial tools capable of directing resources where they will do the most good. The ability to obtain high-value services for persons who need them may engender greater public support for more-universal coverage. The logic is as follows:

- Provider payment reform and federal–state financing reform might be used to better direct medical assistance payments toward coverage of essential services for those who need the assistance most and will receive the highest value from the services.

- When a greater share of medical assistance both goes to essential high-value services and can be shown to do so, the public will place a higher value on medical assistance payments.

- When the public places a higher value on medical assistance payments, there will be greater support for programs to ensure health insurance coverage for lower-income groups.

- Therefore, provider payment reform and federal–state financing reform might be used to attain higher value from medical assistance payments and greater public support for programs to ensure health insurance coverage for lower-income groups.

Thus, the types of reforms we propose for Medicaid provider payment and federal–state financing may be the key to ensuring continued public support for the program and broader reform. This may be achieved through restructuring Medicaid to direct more resources to those most in need of assistance to obtain coverage for basic medical benefits (many in lower-income states) and fewer resources to where they are being used to provide more extensive benefits than are available in many other states (such as personal care services in high-income, high-benefit states).

A corollary to this logic, relating to voters' willingness to accept cost containment for themselves and for the poor, holds implications for the open acknowledgment and acceptability of medical care with more than one standard for access:

- Cost containment (really, cost management) is needed to achieve greater value for dollars spent on insurance coverage for lower-income groups.

- Beyond a fairly minimal level, voter-taxpayers will not accept cost containment for themselves, but they will support more coverage for lower-income groups if it produces greater value for dollars spent.

- Therefore, achieving greater and more valuable insurance coverage for lower-income groups will require imposition of cost containment or management on lower-income groups that does not apply to the typical voter-taxpayers themselves.

Some may decry multiple care-management standards as two-class medicine and say such differential cost containment harms the poor (presumably compared to some ideal alternative, not relative to today's status), and is therefore unacceptable. Nonetheless, the logic here suggests that differential cost containment, far from being a bad thing for the poor, may instead be the pathway to coverage and protection from burdensome medical costs. Making medical care with multiple access levels respectable and truly acceptable, however, will require that the cost containment applied to the poor really be value-oriented, and protect access to care that is truly effective and cost-effective.

Reducing the use of uncostworthy care, then, needs to be an important part of any plan that intends to provide new benefits to new populations and fund them in part from savings on current public spending, rather than entirely out of new taxpayer expenditures.[8] A key question for reform is what mechanism would be used to achieve the goal of reducing government funding of low-value care. Many plans suggest various forms of cost containment and efficiencies (which, as we have noted, are largely unproven to reduce use of low-value care by significantly more than they cost to implement). We suggest that, for reform to be effective, it will be necessary to reduce somehow the flow of funds into the system and let patients and providers then make decisions about the use of limited funds. This can be sought for Medicaid through various strategies in eligibility, benefits, and care management, to be sure, but it is only likely to be truly successful with stronger measures that directly control funds made available through limits on provider payment and federal–state financing. We would focus any discussion of innovations primarily on the rather dry topics of provider payment (such as evidence-based and capitated payment methods) and federal–state financing, because that is how to control most directly the flow of funds while yet leaving room for patient and physician decision-making.

An alternative approach, which has been tried in Oregon (for Medicaid) and the United Kingdom, is to prioritize services in some way and deny payment for anything not meeting approval criteria, hoping that doing so will cut out enough new technology to get close to a budgetary target. Among the many proposals for reform, former U.S. Senator Daschle has suggested the formation of a "Federal Health Board" which would, among its duties, "promote 'high-value' medical care by recommending coverage of those drugs and procedures backed by solid evidence," perhaps along the lines of (an idealized version of) Great Britain's National Institute for Health and Clinical Excellence.[9] This entity would use research evidence to establish guidelines on practice and the use of new technologies. We are, perhaps, much better positioned now to undertake such a plan, after several decades of outcomes and effectiveness research funded by the Agency for Health Care Research and Quality and other entities, than we were in the past. But with an imperfect knowledge base and uncertain medical outcomes, doctors and patients still face the problems of medical decision-making and the inherent tradeoffs of risks of treatment and nontreatment—and the question of whether costs should be considered in such decisions. This issue becomes political when we extend such considerations to decisions on medical insurance coverage or practice guidelines. If one aspires to have a system that provides cost-effective care, one must be willing to consider costs in medical treatment decisions in assessing risks; but this is not generally accepted by some who are vocal in public debates on such issues. So there are both political and knowledge-based limits to what can come from applying comparative-effectiveness research.

Even with good evidence, securing compliance with guidelines would not be an easy task, administratively or politically, because virtually every treatment or drug provides costworthy benefits to some patients. Coverage determinations would have to identify the specific conditions under which any treatment limitation would apply. Nor can we be sure the efforts would, on balance, do more good than harm. To do well would require not only assessing evidence that may be incomplete, debatable, or speculative (and dependent on how new technologies are used in standard practice); it would also require developing explicit cost-effectiveness criteria and effectively assigning a monetary value to health outcomes— something only Oregon has been willing to attempt, and only for its Medicaid population.

We have emphasized the need for Medicaid to work with other payers regarding standards of care. A "Federal Health Board" or other such entity could provide a vehicle for extending this role across the health-care sector if it could be done in a politically acceptable way. The authority assigned to any such board would have to leave room for individual health plans to craft insurance products that fit the groups they serve, using the medical effectiveness and cost-effectiveness information the board produced. Private plans might choose to pay for things that public plans would not; private plans with higher cost-sharing might choose to adopt broader coverage; Medicare might choose different standards than state Medicaid programs. Additionally, individual consumers should be permitted to override collective decisions on value if they attach higher value to and are willing to pay for the care, or to pay extra for insurance that would cover it without a direct or tax subsidy. Making sure such safety valves are in place might be very helpful in allaying anxiety about government controls of medical-care delivery and financing. Because of the great uncertainty about the feasibility of this approach, it seems sensible to proceed cautiously.

Linking payment to evidence of effectiveness, with more generous payment rates set for the more proven treatments, has some advantages over care management programs that are costly to operate, or inflexible coverage rules. We would suggest, then, that state Medicaid programs and other public and private health plans not deny coverage for accepted medical procedures outright, but rather use differential payment rates to guide patients and providers toward more cost-effective treatment decisions. Here again we see benefits from coordinating Medicaid with any new health-care program, and the opportunity for Medicaid programs to be among the first to find ways to implement such reforms.

But true success in reducing uncostworthy care is not something that is going to be accomplished in the next few years, or come easily from applying the latest round of care management buzzwords. Rather, it will occur only when the patient and the doctor at the bedside are comfortable choosing together a course of treatment that provides acceptable and humane care from a set of proven therapies—and are not driven by a technological imperative to seek out the latest expensive test, procedure, or drug that might offer only a small chance of success or improvement in the patient's condition. This may require retraining the next generation of doctors into a profession that values the craftsmanship of achieving the best patient outcomes with the clinical tools proven most effective, rather than the newest, most costly ones. It may require retraining American patients to value the kind of care that focuses on their quality of life and accepts the limitations of affordable technology.

## Using Medicaid to Remove Barriers to Reform

Medicaid could be used as a vehicle, either alone or as a component of a new plan, to help overcome barriers to more universal coverage in the U.S. health-care financing system. Implementing the right changes within Medicaid would make the system more consistent with sound economic principles (pricing services near cost or at competitive rates) and would address issues of efficiency, and of equity for beneficiaries, providers, and taxpayers. As noted below, some offsetting trade-offs would be necessary to compensate the interest groups whose support would be needed. Challenges include:

- Weaning states from dependence on too-low Medicaid provider payment rates (and, in return, providing federal matching funds for a broader population without strict categorical limits)

- Weaning employers and insured workers from excessive federal subsidies on health insurance benefits (by capping tax exclusion for health insurance at some fixed level at or above the cost of an average plan), and avoiding employer efforts to replace mildly subsidized employment-related benefits with heavily subsidized Medicaid benefits

- Weaning safety-net hospital and community health providers from high or supplemental payment rates (and, in return, covering the cost of their uninsured patients directly and with more accountability)

- Adapting the payment system to market factors, using competition to establish payment rates in places where competition can exist and using those competitive rates (as well as research-based Medicare rates) as benchmarks to set payment levels in noncompetitive market areas.

Successful reform will require time to shift resources from the currently entrenched set of providers and services to the new distribution. Given sufficient time for planning and gradual implementation, everyone can make the transition to the new environment without too much sacrifice. Trying to change too quickly, however, could engender political opposition and lead to uncomfortable compromises over meeting key objectives.

# 2

# Making Medicaid Part of National
# Health-Care Reform

Medicaid presents a challenge for any national health-care reform plan because any new program must either overlay or replace the existing program in its fifty manifestations in the states (plus the District of Columbia and U.S. territories). How can Medicaid interface with a new program and the two work together to minimize gaps in coverage and equitable treatment of beneficiaries and providers across programs?

## Issues to Address

Several plans for national health-care reform have been released in recent months, and debate on the topic is active and evolving, with many expecting some form of major legislation to emerge soon.[10] Whether consensus takes weeks, months, or years, our task here is not to provide a comparison or assess the relative merits of any specific proposal, but rather to identify areas where such plans may interface with Medicaid in ways that would require one program to be designed or modified to account for the other. In effect, we are highlighting areas that will need to be given attention in any health-care reform to address the needs of the lower-income uninsured.

The range of possibilities for handling Medicaid in national reform is certainly wide. It could, for instance, be totally ignored by a new program that targets a different population; it could be totally replaced by a program that supersedes it; or it could be made to interface with the new program in some way, perhaps even as a key part of the overall reform effort itself. Congress will have to base its decisions on the kind of health-care system it wants for the future and how much debt or taxes it is willing to add to get there. It would not be wise to ignore Medicaid in any of these cases, however, for several reasons: Medicaid is the starting point for any reform that is to deal with the low-income segment of the population; changes are needed in Medicaid itself (the need for which should be addressed by any program that replaces it); and Medicaid is (or its successor will be) a major part of the health-care financing system. In short, it is important, whatever the composition of programs will be in the future, to provide for the medical-care needs of low-income persons without gaps or inconsistencies that affect their access to care.

Even if we envision addressing the key issues involved in any health-care reform for the low-income population easily and elegantly in a totally new program that replaces Medicaid, we still have to figure out how to get from here to there, and understand what changes will be needed and who will be affected. Given our assessment of reforms currently likely to be viable, we advocate "interfacing" Medicaid with a new program, and we consider how this might be accomplished so as to offer access to some form of subsidy or health insurance to those currently uninsured. We emphasize that we do not advocate such an "interfaced" program as the ideal; indeed, we expect any plan that emerges from the political process to be far from ideal. But awareness of the issues and their significance will help policymakers ground any plan in a realistic understanding of where we are today and what they will need to do to implement a national reform that deals fairly and equitably with Medicaid stakeholders, including recipients, providers, and taxpayers. Here are several areas they will need to address:

- Filling the gaps in eligibility and benefits within a diverse set of state programs to provide greater equity for recipient beneficiaries across states

- Creating the right federal financial incentives for states to curtail or expand Medicaid spending as required

- Ensuring that any changes (particularly eligibility or benefit mandates) do not require imposing a large or inequitable state tax burden (as a percentage of taxpayer income) in any state

- Improving equality across settings and accountability in payments for providers

- Reducing disproportionate share hospital (DSH) payments and other supplemental payments as the number of uninsured persons is reduced (or otherwise replacing them with more accountable payment methods)

- Fast-tracking Medicaid acute-care reforms to provide for implementation ahead of, and in concert with, any broader program to reduce the numbers of uninsured

- Defining the relationship of Medicaid to any new administrative structure.

Of the issues listed, perhaps the most readily identified is the first: the need to account, in program planning, for the wide diversity in eligibility and benefits under state Medicaid and CHIP programs. Any program designed to fill the gaps in coverage, as opposed to replacing existing programs wholesale, will need to recognize the existing interstate differences in the groups remaining uninsured and how those differences are related to the eligibility for existing programs. A blanket-like eligibility expansion program designed to provide a more or less uniform extra layer of additional funding across states could reduce the number of uninsured, but it would not be intended to provide access to everyone and might still leave many uninsured or underinsured. A wood-filler-like program designed to fill the gaps and holes might add on to existing coverage and reach everyone below some specified level of income, but probably would add relatively little in the more generous higher-income states. It would, however, be quite different from the blanket expansion program in how it allocates new resources among the states, reaching much lower in the income distribution to pick up those not covered by Medicaid in the lower-benefit states. Great differences will exist among states, whether the program is limited in some way by income or by eligibility for employer coverage or by categorical requirements, or intended to be available to all as an option.

These differences will need to be dealt with in some way. One could create a rule that draws arbitrary lines among programs—for instance, Medicaid could cover everyone up to 150 percent of the federal poverty level (FPL) for those eligible, CHIP up to 250 percent of the FPL for those eligible, and the new program everyone else, subject to some set of limits. To ensure everyone is covered, one would then have to mandate states to cover under Medicaid and CHIP all those under the specified cutoffs (or else leave low-income uninsured in the low-benefit states). This would be a major change in Medicaid, essentially greatly expanding the mandatory eligibility groups and services. Unless addressed in design with compensating Medicaid financing provisions, such a change would almost surely impose new burdens on the overstressed taxpayers in lower-income, low-benefit states. This disadvantage could be avoided, however, if an alternative matching structure, such as the "Equal-Burden-for-Equal-Benefit" matching structure we have proposed elsewhere, is adopted.[11] EBEB matching rates are specifically constructed so that every state can provide a specified base level of benefit to all poor persons for the same fraction of taxpayer income (or, in some versions, adjusted to provide some progressivity). In short, the EBEB matching would lay a foundation with incentives for states to cover all the poor and financing that would not be disproportionately burdensome in any state if the base coverage for all poor were made mandatory.

Alternatively, one could allow individuals and families to opt into any program for which they are eligible. This would ensure everyone access to (presumably affordable) coverage, even allowing them to choose among qualified existing plans and apply a subsidy in some form. It would, however, also leave states free to curtail their Medicaid and CHIP programs. While prohibiting states from reducing Medicaid and CHIP benefits might prevent this, it would lock in existing inequities in the system, perhaps penalizing those that have made an effort to expand such programs. Though not necessarily grossly inequitable, particularly if the restrictions tend to apply mostly in higher-income states that have taken advantage of the programs, such effects need to be anticipated and considered. A truly neutral subsidy arrangement setting up Medicaid or CHIP as an alternative to other qualified insurance a person might choose might, if possible, be a good idea, but it would definitely shake up Medicaid programs that have previously had a monopoly on generously subsidized coverage.

The point here is that any new program must account for its impacts on both recipient equity and taxpayer equity. To ignore such effects in design takes the risk (at a minimum) of creating unintended inequities among states and their taxpayers and citizens in need of assistance with health-care costs, and perhaps even jeopardizing the political acceptability of the program by alienating some important stakeholders or constituent groups. If Medicaid or CHIP would wither away in the face of better alternatives, its demise would be both good and acceptable. But when any public program shrinks (think of welfare rolls in the Clinton era), there is always a worry that something might be lost.

Let's consider, for a moment, such a possible new program. Assume it would follow the Massachusetts Commonwealth Connector approach, which makes arrangements with existing health-care organizations to offer new managed-care products that meet government specifications. Eligible persons would be offered coverage with a premium determined on a sliding scale and provided with an income-related public subsidy. The program would, of course, face the plan participation and implementation problems Massachusetts has had to contend with and has largely solved. Enrollment would be unpredictable and costs possibly higher than expected—issues with which Massachusetts is still contending. Crowd-out of private insurance would apply here as well. Unlike Commonwealth Connector, however, whose design involved interfacing with only one state's Medicaid program and its local safety-net providers, a national health exchange, or some such entity, would need to interface with fifty state programs, plus a diverse array of CHIP and safety-net payment systems. A seamless interface would be much more difficult to achieve on a national scale, though it might not have to be perfect.

Continuing with our example, let's suppose the national program were simply overlayered upon existing state programs. Separating the new program from Medicaid and CHIP could be accomplished by making it apply to different categorical groups, or different income groups, or different services, or some combination of these. Let's suppose the new program were to focus on acute care (as most recent discussion has been on acute-care coverage of the uninsured, not long-term-care costs), and that it left Medicaid and CHIP to cover those below some percentage of the FPL, with no access to employer-based insurance. Then some distinct groups could be defined to be served by each program. Suppose further that the sliding-scale premium subsidy at its low-income end were set to make it somewhat less attractive to individuals than the existing CHIP program. So, with presumably fewer categorical restrictions, it would attract and serve persons and families not currently covered by public financing.

The question then is, what is the appropriate mix of federal and state financing, and what level of participant cost-sharing is appropriate? While this would undoubtedly be a subject of debate, we can base our discussion on the simple diagram in figure 2-1, which shows coverage for a single hypothetical family with an annual medical cost of $10,000. Our example allows for "affordable" funding through

- federal matching of both Medicaid and CHIP at 60 percent (for this example state)

- participant contribution to premium as a percentage of income, at 2 percent for those at 100–150 percent of the FPL, 3 percent for those at 150–200 percent, 4 percent for those at 200–250 percent, and 5 percent for those above 250 percent of the FPL

- a mandatory employer contribution capped at 10 percent of wages.

FIGURE 2-1

## AN EXAMPLE OF ALLOCATION OF HEALTH INSURANCE COSTS

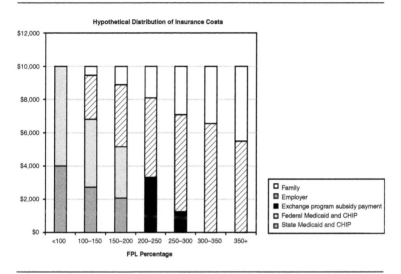

SOURCE: Authors' illustration.

If we were to extend our example to more than the one hypothetical state in the example, we could allow for differential plans and even funding levels across states for the Medicaid and CHIP portions, and for the National Health Exchange portion as well, with states having the ability to expand benefits above average with some limited federal matching and to restrict resources using provider payment rates, as they do now. Our diagram as it stands has the disadvantage both of being based on hypothetical figures and of failing to account for the greater diversity that would exist in practice. It does illustrate, however, that it is possible (for persons at every income level) to divide the costs of insurance in a way that by some measures is not too burdensome for the individual family, the employer, or the government.

An alternative approach with a new program would be simply to add its health plans to the existing mix but to set basic parameters—perhaps through a "Federal Health Board" or "Exchange"—to which all health insurance programs, public and private, would have to conform. States would be free to continue operating their Medicaid and CHIP programs and to set eligibility and benefits. Participants would be able to choose the programs or insurance products they preferred, based on after-subsidy costs and perceived benefits of coverage. Such a health board or exchange would impose some requirements for community rating, nonexcludability, and such, and might oversee one or more new federal "public plan" options, specifying requirements for eligibility and subsidy standards for affordability. The significant implications of these decisions for the federal budget would need to be worked out with Congress.

The more fundamental problem, as noted above, has to do with the level of public support for the overall amount of spending required. From what we have seen in the Medicaid and SCHIP/CHIP experiences, at the state level taxpayer willingness to pay for care for others falls off rather rapidly as the recipient's ability to pay increases, and only continues much above poverty level (in low-income states) or some higher multiple of that (in higher-income states) for the elderly, disabled persons, and children, or when a higher federal subsidy is available (as for CHIP). This seems unlikely to change so long as medical costs grow faster than national income, and especially when national income is growing more slowly than average. With medical costs uncontained, we seem to be moving farther from, rather than closer to, being able to afford universal coverage. Long-term support is not likely to be found for greatly extending eligibility at public expense unless medical costs can be contained and/or the perceived value to taxpayers increased. The implementation of expansive programs would almost certainly lead to great pressure to impose broader and stricter cost containment to maintain political support for the program, and the resistance of the middle class to cost containment might frustrate ambitions for such programs. A more modest Medicaid improvement strategy (with the reach of cost containment limited to the target populations for Medicaid and Medicaid-like programs) may be more politically feasible in the short run.

In all this we want to emphasize the need to pay attention to recipient, taxpayer, and provider equity issues. The approach we have developed here for balancing these stakeholder interests is applicable to any new national health-care reform plan, as well as to Medicaid. It might well be made a part of any such planning process and should help policymakers build on the experiences of Medicaid in developing plans for the future.

## How to Integrate Medicaid with a Massachusetts-Like Plan

The Massachusetts Commonwealth Care plan involves a new state entity, Commonwealth Connector, with the purpose of making sub-sidized insurance available to those previously without public or employer-sponsored coverage, and it has become a model for national health-care reform plans. Among these are several promi-nent plans that call for a health insurance exchange or other such entity to help offer affordable insurance and to cover the uninsured. The attraction is that Massachusetts has apparently found a way to give nearly everyone access to affordable health insurance. There are questions, however, about just what it would take to replicate the model in other states or, indeed, whether it can be replicated in all states. (The rationale for fiscal federalism would imply that no one plan will end up being right for all.) Massachusetts is struggling with the costs of the program, despite its having started with a relatively low percentage of the population uninsured, being a high-income state, receiving unusual federal support thorough a Medicaid waiver, and enforcing a mandate for coverage of the entire population. What federal commitment would it take administratively to make this model work in forty-nine other states with more challenges to over-come? We offer here our suggestions for changes that might help a federal program based on the Massachusetts model fit with Medicaid in different state settings. We include suggestions for dealing with issues such as subsidy levels, eligibility, benefits, program integrity, administrative responsibility, and steps toward implementation.

The possibility of a new, broad, health-care reform program to expand insurance coverage among people at many income levels raises the question of how it might interface with Medicaid in eligibility particularly, but also in coverage and administration. Will the programs overlap? Will people or states be able to choose one program or another? What incentives will be created? Will the new program supplant existing state efforts? Will gaps in eligibility effectively leave some groups out altogether? A new program will require plans to address all these questions.[12]

In addition to raising challenges for existing Medicaid and CHIP programs, such a new program might present opportunities to address, in the process, some of their long-standing problems. While there are many possibilities, we provide some thoughts on how Medicaid and CHIP might be adapted to mesh with such a new program while achieving some of the reforms we have suggested for Medicaid itself.

**Subsidy Levels.** The public subsidy (its form and distribution) is perhaps the central issue to resolve and the element that will provide a defining structure for a new program in the context of existing ones; it is literally the bottom-line issue that asks how serious taxpayers are about slogans they may more easily and cheaply profess than fulfill. The level of subsidy provided for persons at various income levels defines the roles of each program and its relationship to other programs. We turn for a solution to our suggestion for continuity in the federal subsidy across income levels. If one agrees with the idea that the federal subsidy ought to decline continuously as the income of the individual goes up, it remains only to set the levels of subsidy that reflect the preferences of federal voters, determine who else will pay, and then pick the best administrative structure to support each program.

We identify in concept the following groups but do not provide precise definitions, which must be developed in the policy process.

- **Group I: Full public subsidy.** This group is for persons without the means to contribute to premiums for their own insurance. It might include those below the federal poverty level or some multiple of the FPL. For simplicity's sake, let us assume this is 100 percent of the FPL.

- **Group II: Nominal premiums.** Members of this group are able to contribute some amount toward medical premiums, but not enough to constitute a significant portion of costs. Again for simplicity, let us assume their income is at 100–200 percent of the FPL.

- **Group III: Meaningful premiums.** Persons in this group can contribute in a meaningful way to the cost of their insurance, but because wages are low and costs high, theirs will be a small share. Let us assume they are at 200–300 percent of the FPL.

- **Group IV: Modest standard subsidy.** This group does not require a subsidy to obtain access to health care. Rather, as a means of encouraging coverage, most employed persons in it would get the standard subsidy implicit in tax treatment of employer-sponsored insurance. Let us assume this is everyone over 300 percent of the FPL. It may make sense to cap the subsidy amount at some multiple of the cost of a standard plan, to avoid providing an open-ended subsidy to even very high-income Americans, as the current tax structure does.

Whatever the broad group to be covered, it is important that it be partitioned in a sensible way to ensure a clearly specified coverage and subsidy for all those involved. Lumping together groups with different needs to receive the same subsidized coverage will defeat the purpose of reform.

**Eligibility.** One key goal of an exchange-type program is to fill the gaps and create seamless coverage for all. The SCHIP/CHIP experience provides evidence of the dangers lurking in this endeavor. Even some high-income states appear to require higher federal subsidies to expand benefits, but they need a cap of, say, 200 percent of the poverty level or somewhere near it to avoid overshooting if the subsidies are too generous. Such a cap seems plausible, as many states currently provide Medicaid and/or CHIP up to this level. We do not, however, see Medicaid as a good vehicle for people with incomes above about 200 percent of the FPL, as state taxpayer willingness to provide support falls off and individual ability to pay increases more rapidly above this level. A program better geared to significant cost-sharing and minimum state financial participation is needed. State administration may not be appropriate if the state contribution is small.

The question, then, is how to ensure that states do their part to cover those up to the income level at which beneficiaries can get by with the more modest subsidies paid directly to consumers (through an exchange-type subsidy arrangement, tax incentives, or vouchers for insurance purchases). One possibility would be to have the new program provide the full consumer subsidies that individuals would need to procure the standard insurance. But then states would have an incentive to curtail Medicaid eligibility, and let the new program take over responsibility for much of the low-income population—a problem that might be addressed by mandating that states provide Medicaid eligibility to persons below some specified percentage of the poverty level. As federal taxpayers may be more interested in seeing that everyone has coverage than in prescribing just what benefits should be provided or how much providers should be paid within each state's health-care delivery system, there is some rationale for a federal mandate on eligibility that does not necessarily extend to benefits or provider payment rates or methods.

All this suggests that the boundary between the new program and Medicaid eligibility could be mandated as part of the new program, with states having new obligations to cover everyone up to the cut-off level (as a percentage of the FPL, or of the cost of living–adjusted FPL, which could vary by eligibility group), and the exchange-type program having responsibility for everyone above that point. Although we suggest a partitioning of responsibility for administering programs for these groups, we also suggest continuity of the subsidy schedule across groups. This is to ensure each beneficiary's subsidy never changes appreciably with small changes in income, even if it means moving from Medicaid or CHIP to an exchange-sponsored plan. This will help ensure smooth coverage and subsidy transitions as individual economic circumstances change.

The key challenge to making Medicaid mesh with an exchange-type program is ensuring continuity in the subsidy across beneficiary income levels. That is, there should be no sharp drops—no notches—in the subsidy as the beneficiary's income increases. Accomplishing this should provide some measure of vertical equity and also avoid the types of situations (that now exist) in which people have an incentive to decline to pursue employment opportunities in order to maintain Medicaid benefits, or to decline employer-based coverage to get the more heavily subsidized Medicaid benefits. But the notion of smoothing the relationship between subsidy and Medicaid eligibility will be important, whatever arrangement is put in place for those who are not subsidized to more than a modest extent.

**Benefits.** Medicaid coverage is typically more comprehensive than private insurance. This makes sense for Medicaid's most vulnerable populations with little ability to pay any significant expenses themselves. However, since higher-income groups can afford to pay more around the edges for uncovered services (such as dental care or eyeglasses), plans to cover them can logically call for a less comprehensive benefit package. In a public choice context, this may help engender support among a public that is unwilling to pay full freight for those recipients less in need. It makes sense for both benefits and the public subsidy to be less for persons above traditional Medicaid income eligibility levels.

**Integrity in Payment and Coverage Decisions.** It is critically important that health-care reformers pay attention to provider payment issues and incentives for provision of high-value care, and to avoid provision of care that is not worth what it costs. Providers working through the legislative process sometimes undermine, through many preferential exceptions, the integrity of well-founded and objective payment methodologies. The growth over time of such exceptions, and the difficulties of removing preferences once granted, should provide a lesson to any new program: Be careful not to allow the discussions over any new system to be dominated by provider views on what treatments are "needed" or not needed, or by provider groups' claims of being underpaid. Medicaid is all about allocating money to providers, and the distribution of funds is largely determined by the rules on coverage, payment rates, and methods. The integrity of the payment process depends on developing and maintaining clear standards for provider payment built on objective criteria not subject to manipulation by any of the players through the political process. While Congress plays a very appropriate role in setting public program budgets, there are good reasons for it to step back and defer to experts on the detailed tasks of rate-setting and coverage determination.[13] In payment and coverage issues (which can affect the relative benefits to different providers or health plans), program reforms should be designed to reflect principles—such as those we suggest below—rather than specific requirements.

**Administrative Responsibility.** A key decision for any national program that follows the Massachusetts model is the extent to which states would administer it. Is the vision one in which different states might be permitted or encouraged to do things differently, or will programs be required to conform to some single model for the whole country? Two considerations are important in making this decision. One is to determine where the expertise and organizational capabilities lie, and the other is to determine where the financing will come from. On the one hand, there are dangers in separating administrative responsibility too far from expertise on local health-care systems and plans. On the other, separating responsibility and decisions too far from the primary source of funds may also carry risks. Our analysis indicates most new financing to support coverage of higher-income groups will need to come from federal rather than state sources. Since putting the states in charge of programs to which they contribute very little will not create the desired incentives for financial responsibility, overall financial responsibility for benefits, coverage, and contracting should be kept at the federal level. States could continue to operate Medicaid and CHIP plans that would take full responsibility for persons below specified income levels for each categorical group. The federal government could choose to develop a fee-for-service public-sector plan (a major administrative task) or contract for a publicly sponsored and subsidized managed plan that meets specific cost and access requirements as a fallback for those not in private plans.

**Initial Steps.** Altogether, major reform is conceivable if costs can be controlled and resources found. Changes may not all need to happen at once; if resources are scarce, a phased approach, with specific checkpoints to evaluate mistakes and make corrections, may be more politically acceptable than an all-at-once implementation. Given the perilous nature of the health reform journey, it is asking too much to expect the perfect map; we need, rather, a sense of the general direction in which to go and a plan for midcourse correction. We would suggest as initial steps using changes in Medicaid and CHIP to move national reform in the right direction and create a foundation for future changes that would lead to the goal of more universal coverage while achieving some of the equity and efficiency goals we have promoted in this work.

### Principles for Reform

Although we do not suggest specifics of Medicaid reform here (they will be covered in our forthcoming book),[14] we next offer a few guiding principles to help policymakers sort out the innumerable possibilities involved in reforming Medicaid, CHIP, and any new program to provide health insurance coverage to lower-income persons with the help of public funds.

- **Principle of Interstate Equity: Public programs should promote greater (if not complete) equality of treatment for beneficiaries and taxpayers across states.** While perfect equity may not be possible, future programs ought to do a better job of making benefits equally available to all in similar economic circumstances regardless of state of residence; adjusting federal matching to provide equity for taxpayers will also be needed to bring Medicaid spending in low-benefit states up toward national averages. Policymakers should focus on measures such as medical assistance per poor person and the share of taxpayer income devoted to program funding in every state. Both recipients and taxpayers should be able to count on treatment that is equitable relative to similarly situated persons in other states.

- **Principle of Continuity of Subsidy: The public subsidy for health insurance coverage should decrease in a continuous way with increases in the income of the individual or family.** This principle serves two purposes, one for recipients and one for taxpayers. First, recipients ought to be assured that they will receive more assistance when their incomes are less, and that benefits are not going to be suddenly cut off if their incomes reach some threshold. This continuity in subsidy ought to be applied as seamlessly as possible across Medicaid, CHIP, new programs, and employer-based coverage. Second, this principle reflects continuity in voter-donor preferences for meeting the needs of those who need assistance most. Funds for these recipients are more likely to go for basic medical services that may do the most to improve health. In sum, following this principle should both improve equity and help direct resources to where they will do the most good—thereby enhancing the value of the program to the taxpayers who pay for it.

- **Principle of Equality of Payment across Settings: Payment methods should provide for equality of payment of providers for similar services by type and setting.**

Medicaid currently pays some providers more favorably than others, essentially imposing a tax on those less favored providers who are willing to continue to provide services at Medicaid rates and subsidizing non-Medicaid activities or incomes of those who receive more favorable rates. These differentials are particularly problematic when providers are allowed to classify themselves for payment purposes. Special payment arrangements such as DSH payments, cost reimbursement for rural hospitals, and higher payment for physician office visits in hospital-affiliated practices are neither efficient nor equitable. The rationale for such payments will disappear if and when standard Medicaid payment rates are made adequate and the numbers of uninsured (and amounts of associated uncompensated care) are reduced. Access to care under public programs could be improved, at no greater cost, if Medicaid and other programs did a better job of paying adequately by the service delivered. Providers should be able to count on standard, equitable payments for services delivered, regardless of the delivery setting.

- **Principle of Claims-Based Accountability: Payment methods not based on claims should be eliminated and replaced with other systems to account for use of funds.** Although most Medicaid spending is documented by medical claims that report what service was delivered and who received it, there are exceptions, including DSH payments, cost reimbursement of critical-access hospitals, and medical education payments. These should be replaced by more accountable, claims-based programs to support Medicaid-affected safety-net providers. Except for competitive managed-care contracts or Diagnosis-Related-Group (DRG)–based hospital claims (where case characteristics determine payment), claims should be sufficiently detailed to represent the use of resources as do RBRVS relative values for the services provided. This would preclude encounter-based claims for professional services where a flat visit rate is applied without reference to the content of that visit, as reported by procedure code. Taxpayers should be able to count on proper accountability for program funds spent.

- **Principle of Provider Network Control: Publicly funded health insurance programs should exercise greater control over their provider networks, similar to that applied in private managed-care plans.** This second principle for accountability is directed at reducing payments to fly-by-night providers of questionable services, organized billing scams, and providers who consistently abuse their billing privileges. Medicaid (and Medicare) fee-for-service programs essentially allow participation of any willing provider. These programs need the greater authority and resources to screen providers for participation, exclude providers based on performance, and reward providers for superior performance, or to otherwise select capable, well-performing providers and exclude others, through, for example, a competitive bidding process.

- **Principle of Economy in Production of Health: Public funding should favor those services for which there is evidence of better health outcomes.** Public programs and their payment systems should provide systems, incentives, and controls to promote the use of effective and cost-effective services. Whether achieved by coverage limits, care management (with the costs of the care management itself subject to watch), or payment incentives, the program should discourage provision of and eliminate payment for services that do not have an expected health impact whose value exceeds their cost.

- **Principle of Objective, Nonpolitical Coverage and Rate-Setting Decisions: Both coverage and rate-setting decisions should be made on a technical basis by objective decision-makers with the requisite expertise.** Detailed coverage decisions should be made by persons with medical expertise who do not have a financial interest in the decision—this means trained medical experts not currently engaged in providing the services under consideration. Similarly, payment rate decisions should be made on a technical basis by health economists and/or actuaries with detailed knowledge of the payment methodologies and economics of the delivery system. For these functions, Congress may choose to engage existing organizations, AHRQ, MedPAC, CMS, and/or or a new organizational entity as has been proposed by Daschle, Emanuel, and others.[15] Congress, which lacks the needed expertise and is too accessible to the views of well-represented narrow interests, can readily do its job of representing the public interest if it confines its input to *who should be covered, for what general services,* and *the budget to be made available.*

- **Principle of Value-Based Cost Containment: Public programs should not pay more than necessary to obtain the supply of services needed by program beneficiaries.** Medicaid, more than other payers, restricts funding to providers, but much more could be done to ensure the program is not paying more than necessary and is not paying for services that are not worth their cost. In various parts of Medicaid we still see such practices as differential payment for similar services, cost-based reimbursement, and use of brand-name drugs where generics might suffice. Providers will always seek higher payments and more opportunities to provide services, but only by reducing the flow of funds into the health-care system will the use of services not worth their cost be eliminated. And at the national level, it is only by containing costs that our nation will be able to afford to extend medical-care coverage to all of its citizens.

- **Principle of Automatic Economic Adjustment: Public programs for lower-income persons should provide for automatic adjustments to the economic cycle.** In economic adversity, state revenues decrease at the very time additional funds are needed to support the greater number of persons in need. While states might do a better job of building and managing their reserve funds, a federal solution is logical. States should be able to count on not having to wait for changes in federal policy to receive additional federal funds in times of economic downturn. Similarly, in times of economic growth, taxpayers should be able to count on the federal payments to return to normal and provide savings that will be needed in the future.

- **Principle of Partitioned Responsibility: Any reform program should clearly partition the responsibility to provide for everyone to whom the plan applies.** In mathematics, a partition is a collection of non-overlapping subsets that comprise an entire set, without any gaps. For Medicaid reform as part of national health-care reform, partitioned responsibility means specifying in the plan what will happen to everyone so that no one is left unprovided for by Medicaid, CHIP, Medicare, employer coverage, safety-net providers, or any new program. This requires attending to the interfaces among programs or program components in any reform plan.

Principles have an important role to play in the reform debate. While one can argue over just what principles should apply and how, they provide a means of ensuring some fundamental values are accounted for in the reform process, and that any product will be designed to achieve some clearly recognized objectives. The alternative to such a principled approach—an alternative that apparently is being much followed in Washington these days—is to try to reach consensus among the special interests of providers, suppliers, health plans, and those recipient groups with visible representation. A decision process that seeks the consent of providers and insurers would seem much less likely to balance appropriately the interests of voters and program beneficiaries with those of the providers. Nor is it likely to produce an outcome that will provide adequately for equity, accountability, and cost containment. While provider input is needed to keep program plans grounded in the real world, Congress and the Obama administration would do well to return to principles such as these when making decisions on health-care reform.

# 3

# Thinking Strategically about Reform

At the strategic level, perhaps the most important health-care reform choices have to do with controlling the considerable reallocation of resources that will necessarily occur with any major national reform. It is worth pausing to think about what shifts in resources are intended, how they are to take place, and what controls will be imposed upon them.

Hadley and colleagues provide an analysis and estimate of the net resource cost required to cover all uninsured persons in the United States.[16] They estimate the net additional resource cost to be about $123 billion annually. This amount would increase U.S. health-care spending by 5.1 percent, or 0.8 percent of the gross domestic product (GDP). While costs would depend on whatever program were adopted, this is likely to be a lower-bound estimate, as program costs may well exceed real resource costs due to crowd-out enrollment by those otherwise insured, supply-side price increases (perhaps ratified politically to gain support for the program), and other inefficiencies. Since Hadley estimates the total cost of covering those now uninsured at about $299 billion annually, we would expect a program that provided coverage just to those persons to have expenditures approximating at least 65 percent of Medicare, or about 153 percent of total federal and state Medicaid acute-care expenditures—a large program by any measure.[17] While a significant share of the program could be funded with beneficiary premiums and cost-sharing, much would still be needed from public funds that ideally could be partly offset by recovering the cost of charity and bad-debt care currently received by the uninsured. Even so, such a program is probably too big to take on all at once.

An incremental approach to expanding coverage of the uninsured may be advisable.

The public choice model, though focused on Medicaid in our discussion so far, provides a framework for thinking about broader health-care reform. One central challenge for broader reform is the apparent unwillingness of American voter-taxpayers to pay higher taxes to fund additional health benefits for others, particularly those outside Medicaid categorical eligibility groups and above Medicaid income levels for eligibility. So another challenge will be to find a way to satisfy the voter-taxpayers that they are getting value for their medical assistance tax dollars and a fair shake for themselves. One way to do this would be to get a transitional subsidy to the lower middle class in place first, and then expand Medicaid and CHIP to fill the gap. This approach runs counter to the idea that the neediest should be tended to first, but it may nonetheless have some political advantages. Of course, an all-at-once strategy might work if the financial and political means can be found for everyone to be brought onboard for the ride.

The contrary view, and one we think is more practical, is that of an incremental process, with Medicaid and CHIP the logical first areas to receive increased funding. We would suggest the priorities outlined above could be followed, with initial efforts directed to expanding Medicaid eligibility in lower-income states through extension of the mandatory eligibility groups, coupled with additional funding through enhanced federal matching for lower-income persons by categorical groups, with children most favored. This initial step would even out Medicaid eligibility so everyone up to some specified percentage of the federal poverty level (varying by categorical group) would be covered. We would suggest this is the best use of any down payment on health-care reform, such as that proposed by President Obama. It would lay the groundwork for a federal program, perhaps along the lines of the Massachusetts model or a voucher-for-coverage subsidy, which could then begin to extend some of the same principles we have suggested to a new program and new eligibility groups and to ensure health insurance coverage for more of the population.

Unless there is a major shift in voter preferences, cost savings (in the form of lower growth in spending than otherwise would have occurred) should be a key element of any financing plan. Any such plan should be structured so that cost containment targets for public spending must be reached *before* expanding eligibility; this would avoid the situation that has occurred with state Medicaid waiver programs that are funded prospectively, with certain added costs to be financed with presumed but uncertain savings that may never materialize. Lobbyists are highly skilled at proposing schemes to spend more now on new program benefits, coverage, payment rates, preventive services, or care management methods, with the promise of unproven future savings. We can only hope our elected representatives are equally skilled at avoiding the trap of proposals that entail "certain costs and uncertain savings," and that they learn to rely on the Congressional Budget Office and other objective sources to debunk such plans and fairly assess the cost-saving prospects of new proposals.

In the end, a major reform would require major shifts in resources. Financing of the new program would likely come from a variety of sources, such as beneficiary cost-sharing, the ending of DSH and other supplemental payments, new federal spending, and a cap on the tax deductibility of health insurance premiums. Such reform may seek to replace the less accountable segments of the program, particularly anything not requiring the documentation of detailed medical claims showing precisely what was delivered and to whom. The long-term objectives would be to get everyone an insurance card so all medical costs could be monitored through claims, eliminate the less-accountable forms of safety-net funding (such as DSH, Health Resources and Services Administration [HRSA] grants, and cost-reimbursed hospitals of various types), and provide incentives for cost containment to providers and health plans. A master plan for these shifts and a plan for monitoring progress would be very important, whether the reform in the end were large or small.

The next steps in health-care reform ought to be designed to deal with the fundamental problems of inequity, inefficiency, and unaccountability in our current system. Yet they must also be responsive to the democratic process and consistent with resources that can reasonably be made available. The changes needed in our health-care system cannot be made overnight. If one thinks of all that really needs to be changed—the major shifts in financing, the major changes in medical practice, and the development of supporting information technology—it is not unreasonable to expect it to take ten years or more. We think it makes sense for policymakers to think very carefully about what we really want for our health-care system, to reach some public consensus on a long-term goal, and then to put in place a structure that will carry us through what (even with a clear goal in mind) will have to be a long, slow process of reform. Medicaid reform should be a central part of the first stage of any major national health-care reform program. Such a first step is needed to ensure reform that addresses some important immediate needs and also eliminates some of the most troublesome barriers to further progress.

# Notes

1. By our estimates, even after adjusting for geographic cost differences, Medicaid payments per person below 125 percent of the federal poverty level differ by a factor of more than 3 (that is, the average benefit in the highest state is three times that in the lowest state) and 1.47 from the first to third quartile (that is, the seventeenth-ranked state has benefits 47 percent higher than the thirty-fourth ranked state, District of Columbia included). Grannemann and Pauly 2009.

2. Grannemann and Pauly 2009.

3. Pagan and Pauly 2006.

4. An example is recent calls for a public plan option in national health reform.

5. Hadley et al. 2008.

6. Blendon et al. 2008.

7. See Marmor, Oberlander, and White 2009 for a discussion of cost control options consistent with this view.

8. We use the terms "costworthy" and "uncostworthy" in the sense of Menzel (1983), as care that is or is not worth its cost.

9. Daschle with Greenberger and Lambrew 2008, 171–72.

10. Among discussions of the issue are Obama 2008, Daschle et al. 2008, Baucus 2008, and the Healthy Americans Act, a bill sponsored by Senator Ron Wyden, a Democrat from Oregon, and others. Also see Emanuel 2008.

11. Grannemann and Pauly 2009.

12. The task of integration would differ if the reform were to be based on some model other than that in Massachusetts, such as one that relied more on vouchers for purchase of private insurance or less on mandates; but these considerations help to make more concrete some key issues in Medicaid policy.

13. Some of these reasons are discussed in Daschle et al. 2008, 116–29.

14. Grannemann and Pauly 2009.

15. Daschle et al. 2008; Emanuel 2008.

16. Hadley et al. 2008.

17. Based on CMS Office of the Actuary estimates of 2008 Medicare expenditures of $462 billion (Boards of Trustees 2009, 2), and a StateHealthFacts.org FY2007 estimate of Medicaid acute-care expenditures of $194.8 billion (Kaiser Family Foundation 2009).

# References

Baucus, Max. 2008. Call to Action Health Reform 2009. November 12. http://finance.senate.gov/healthreform2009/finalwhitepaper.pdf (accessed April 29, 2009).

Blendon, Robert J., Drew E. Altman, John M. Benson, Mollyann Brodie, Tami Buhr, Claudia Deane, and Sasha Buscho. 2008. Voters and Health Care Reform in the 2008 Presidential Election. *New England Journal of Medicine* 359 (19): 2050–61. http://content.nejm.org/cgi/content/full/359/19/2050. Supplementary material at http://content.nejm.org/cgi/data/NEJMsr0807717/DC1/1 (accessed April 29, 2009).

Boards of Trustees of the Federal Hospital Insurance and Federal Supplementary Medical Insurance Trust Funds. 2009. *Annual Report of the Boards of Trustees of the Federal Hospital Insurance and Federal Supplementary Medical Insurance Trust Funds.* Washington, D.C.: Government Printing Office.

Daschle, Tom, with Scott S. Greenberger and Jeanne M. Lambrew. 2008. *Critical: What We Can Do about the Health-Care Crisis.* New York: St. Martins Press.

Emanuel, Ezekiel J. 2008. *Healthcare, Guaranteed: A Simple, Secure Solution for America.* New York: PublicAffairs.

Grannemann, Thomas W., and Mark V. Pauly. (forthcoming) 2009. *Medicaid Everyone Can Count On.* Washington, D.C.: AEI Press.

Hadley, Jack, John Holahan, Teresa Coughlin, and Dawn Miller. 2008. *Covering the Uninsured in 2008: A Detailed Examination of Current Costs and Sources of Payment, and Incremental Costs of Expanding Coverage.* Prepared for the Kaiser Commission on Medicaid and the Uninsured and the Henry J. Kaiser Family Foundation. August. http://www.kff.org/uninsured/upload/7809.pdf (accessed April 29, 2009).

Kaiser Family Foundation. 2009. *Distribution of Medicaid Spending on Acute Care, FY2007.* Based on data from Centers for Medicare and Medicaid Services-64 reports, March 2009. StateHealthFacts.org.

http://statehealthfacts.org/comparetable.jsp?ind=179&cat=4 (accessed May 20, 2009).

Marmor, Theodore, Jonathan Oberlander, and Joseph White. 2009. "The Obama Administration's Options for Health Care Cost Control: Hope vs. Reality," *Annals of Internal Medicine* 150 (7): 485–89.

Menzel, Paul T. 1983. *Medical Costs, Moral Choices: A Philosophy of Health Care Economics in America.* New Haven, Conn.: Yale University Press.

Obama, Barack. 2008. Affordable Health Care for All Americans: The Obama-Biden Plan. *Journal of the American Medical Association* 300 (16): 1927–28.

Pagan, Jose, and Mark Pauly. 2006. Community Level Uninsurance and the Unmet Needs of Insured and Uninsured Adults. *Health Services Research* 41 (3 pt. 1): 788–803.

# About the Authors

**Thomas W. Grannemann** is associate regional administrator for Medicare Financial Management and Fee for Service Operations in the Boston Regional Office of the Centers for Medicare and Medicaid Services. His research interests include Medicaid financing, hospital costs, long-term care, physician productivity, provider payment methods, and worker's compensation. Previously, Dr. Grannemann was a senior economist at Mathematica Policy Research, Inc., where his work involved design and analysis of major national Medicare and Medicaid demonstration projects. He has also served as chief of the Bureau of Economic Analysis and Rate Setting Policy with the State of New Hampshire Office of Medicaid Business and Policy. For several years, Dr. Grannemann taught health economics, health policy, and public finance at the University of Colorado's Graduate School of Public Affairs and managed his own research and consulting business, Andover Economic Evaluation. He is the author of numerous publications on Medicaid, Medicare, and health-care reform topics. Dr. Grannemann holds a Ph.D. in economics from Northwestern University.

**Mark V. Pauly** is Bendheim Professor in the Department of Health Care Management, Professor of Health Care Management, Insurance and Risk Management, and Business and Public Policy at the Wharton School and Professor of Economics in the School of Arts and Sciences at the University of Pennsylvania. He is also an adjunct scholar of the American Enterprise Institute. Dr. Pauly is an active member of the Institute of Medicine and serves on the national advisory committees for the National Institutes of Health's National

Center for Research Resources, the National Academy of Sciences' Committee to Study the Veterinary Workforce, and the National Vaccine Advisory Commission. He is a co-editor-in-chief of the *International Journal of Health Care Finance and Economics* and an associate editor of the *Journal of Risk and Uncertainty*. A former commissioner on the Physician Payment Review Commission, Dr. Pauly has also served on the advisory committee of the Agency for Health Care Research and Quality and the Medicare Technical Advisory Panel.